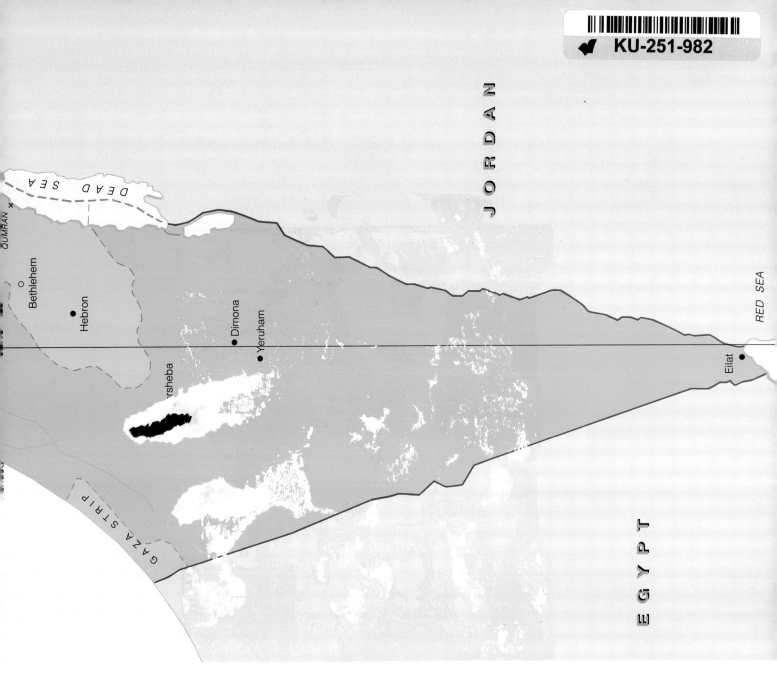

JORDAN

DEAD SEA

QUMRAN ×

Bethlehem ○

● Hebron

● Dimona

rsheba

Yeruham ●

GAZA STRIP

EGYPT

RED SEA

Eilat ●

DISPUTED TERRITORIES

The three areas denoted by dotted lines
are disputed as follows:

GAZA STRIP – between Israel and Palestinians
GOLAN HEIGHTS – between Israel and Syria
WEST BANK – between Israel and Palestinians

Note: disputed territories are marked on this map,
but not on the smaller maps within the book

PALESTINIAN NATIONAL AUTHORITY

○ denotes town controlled by Palestinian National
Authority since 1994 (Jericho) or 1995 (6 other
towns in West Bank)

915. 694

**Books are to be returned on or before
the last date below**

16 APR 2002

2 1 AUG 2002

-5 JUN 2003

21 APR 2004

24 MAY 2004

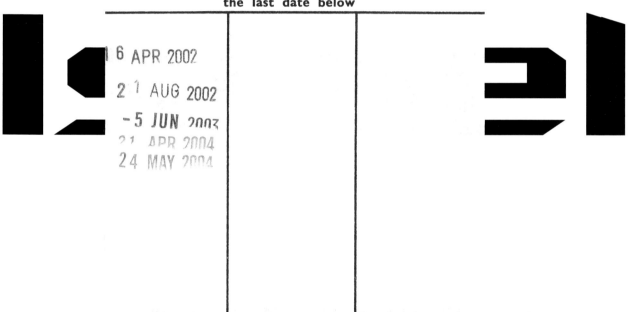

LIBREX —

MACDONALD YOUNG BOOKS

First published in 1997 by Macdonald Young Books
An imprint of Wayland Publishers Ltd
© Macdonald Young Books 1997

Macdonald Young Books
61 Western Road
Hove
East Sussex
BN3 1JD

Design and typesetting Roger Kohn Designs
Commissioning editor Debbie Fox
Editor Diana Russell
Picture research Valerie Mulcahy
Illustration János Márffy

Special thanks to Melvin and Anita Cohen; the staff of the
Public Affairs Department, Embassy of Israel; Shayla Walmsley
of BIPAC (Britain Israel Public Affairs Centre); the library
and office staff of the Oxford Centre for Hebrew and
Jewish studies.

We are grateful to the following for permission
to reproduce photographs:
Front Cover: Richard T Nowitz *above;*
ASAP (Rafael Macia) *below;*
ASAP Israel, pages 7 (Lev Borodulin), 25 (Rafi Magnes),
27 *right* (David Rubinger), 36 (Kenneth Fischer), 37 *above*
(Michael Altschul), 38 (Lev Borodulin), 39 (Eiten Simanor);
J Allan Cash, pages 14, 26; Stephanie Colasanti, pages 21,
28; Bruce Coleman, page 40 (Mark N Boulton); Colorific! page
29 (Sylvain Grandadam); Robert Harding Picture Library,
pages 11 (E Simanor), 15 (ASAP/Israel Talby), 37 *below*
(E Simanor); The Hutchison Library, pages 30 (Tony Souter),
34 (Robert Francis); Impact Photos, pages 8 (Christophe
Bluntzer), 20 *above* (Mark Cator), 24 (John Cole); Katz
Pictures, page 33 (Ricki Rosen/Saba/REA Israel, Ramat Gan
10/93 Magahori & Legziel Diamond Company); Magnum,
pages 9 *above* (Fred Mayer), 10 *above* and *below* (Dennis
Stock), 18 *above* (Micha Bar Am), 22 (Fred Mayer); Richard T
Nowitz, page 19; Christine Osborne Pictures, pages 13 *below,*
18; Panos Pictures, page 27 *left* (Penny Tweedie); Rex
Features, page 43 (Milner Moshe/Sipa Press); Tony Stone
Images, pages 16/17 (Alan Smith); Sygma, page 20 *below*
(L Gilbert); Topham Picturepoint, pages 23, 31, 42,
(M Lipchitz); TRIP, pages 9 *below* (J Arnold), 32 (A Tovy);
Weizmann Institute, page 35 (Miki Koren);
Zefa Pictures, page 41.

The statistics given in this book are the most up to date
available at the time of going to press

Printed in Hong Kong by Wing King Tong

A CIP catalogue record for this book is available from
the British Library

ISBN: 0 7500 2266 3

C O N T E N T S

Words that are explained in the glossary are printed in
SMALL CAPITALS the first time they are mentioned in the text.

✡ INTRODUCTION

More than 3,000 years ago, Jewish people lived in the land of Israel in the Middle East. When the Romans conquered the area ten centuries later, the Jews were dispersed throughout the world. The land was later ruled by other peoples, such as Arabs and OTTOMAN TURKS.

The scattered Jewish communities suffered hatred and persecution in many countries. At the end of the 19th century, the ZIONIST movement was set up to help organize their return to the same area of the Middle East, then called Palestine.

During the Second World War, 6 million Jews were killed in the Nazi HOLOCAUST. As a result, thousands of survivors joined other Jews in Palestine, and together they campaigned for the establishment of a national homeland. In 1947, the United Nations voted in favour of the division of Palestine into two states. Disagreement over this proposal led to the War of Independence in 1948, which was followed by the establishment of the state of Israel. Since then, Israel has found itself at war four more times (1956, 1967, 1973, 1982) with neighbouring Arab countries who were opposed to the creation of the new state. In 1979, Egypt signed a peace treaty with Israel and this was followed in 1994 by peace with Jordan. A comprehensive peace agreement for the region is now closer and

▼ *Jerusalem, the capital of Israel, is more than 3,000 years old. The Western Wall was once part of the ancient Jewish temple. Churches and mosques represent Christianity and Islam.*

the future of the country seems more secure.

In the half century since the state was founded, Israel has absorbed Jewish immigrants from all over the world. There are also significant Christian and Moslem minorities in the country, whose religious freedom is guaranteed by the state. Over the last 50 years, Israeli governments have built schools, hospitals and good transport links. They have also developed agriculture, industry and tourism. In this book, you can find out about these successes and about the challenges that the country still faces.

▶ *A Hebrew fragment from the Dead Sea Scrolls, discovered in 1947 in the Qumran caves, where they had lain for 2,000 years.*

▼ *Tel Aviv-Yafo is the entertainment, business and tourist centre of Israel.*

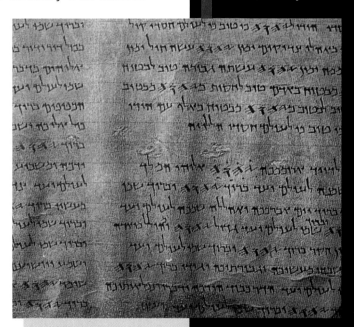

ISRAEL AT A GLANCE

- Area: 28,000 square kilometres
- Population (1996): 5,716,000
- Population density: 204 people per sq km
- Capital: Jerusalem, population 579,800 (1995)
- Other main cities (1995): Tel Aviv-Yafo 355,200; Haifa 247,000; Rishon Le Zion 160,200; Petah Tikva 152,000
- Highest mountain: Hermon, 2,814 metres
- Longest river: Jordan, 320 kilometres
- Official languages: Hebrew, Arabic, English
- Major religions: Judaism, Islam and Christianity
- Currency: Shekel, written as NIS
- Economy: Both agriculture and industry
- Major resources: Minerals from the Dead Sea
- Major products: Citrus fruits, high-tech equipment
- Major exports: Fruit, flowers, polished diamonds, electronic equipment, phosphates
- Environmental problems: Water shortage, increasing pollution, traffic density

THE LANDSCAPE

Israel is long and narrow, measuring only 470 km from north to south and up to 135 km east to west. It has land borders with Lebanon, Syria, Jordan and Egypt. Israel has an amazing variety of landscape for such a tiny country. In the far north, the snow-capped Mount Hermon towers to a height of 2,814 m. In stark contrast, the Dead Sea, at the southern end of the Jordan valley, lies 400 m below sea level. It is the lowest point on earth.

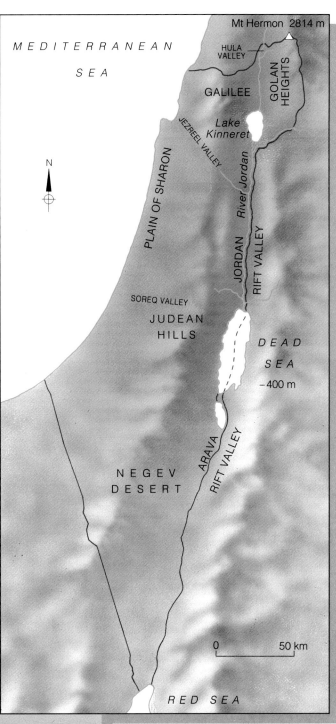

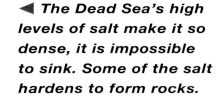

◄ **The Dead Sea's high levels of salt make it so dense, it is impossible to sink. Some of the salt hardens to form rocks.**

There are four main geographical regions. The first is the coastal plain which runs parallel to the Mediterranean Sea. Fertile farmland borders the coast and extends up to 40 km inland. This is the most densely populated region in the country.

The Golan Heights make up the second region, originally formed by ancient volcanic eruptions. This area includes the limestone hills of Galilee, ranging from 500 to 1,200 m above sea level.

The third region is the Jordan Rift valley

◀ *Mount Hermon straddles the borders of Israel, Lebanon and Syria. The snow-capped mountain is excellent for winter skiing. In the foreground is Upper Galilee, where there is good farmland.*

KEY FACTS

● At 28,000 sq km, Israel is about the same size as Wales, or the state of New Jersey in the USA.

● A car trip from Metullah, the most northerly town in Israel, to Eilat in the south can be completed in just 9 hours.

● At 212 m below sea level, Lake Kinneret is the lowest freshwater lake in the world.

● The Dead Sea covers an area of 1,000 sq km.

● The Negev takes up half of the country's land area, yet only 7% of the population live there.

and the Arava, part of the great Syrian-African Rift which split the earth's crust millions of years ago. The River Jordan is fed by streams in the Mount Hermon area. It flows south through the Rift and the Hula valley, descending over 700 m during its 300-km journey through Lake Kinneret (also called the Sea of Galilee or Lake Tiberias) before emptying into the Dead Sea.

The Negev is the fourth region. It is a huge triangle of land in the south of Israel. At its tip lies the Red Sea port of Eilat. The landscape of the arid desert is breathtaking, with sheer cliffs of coloured sandstone, bare craggy peaks, vast craters and dry river beds known as WADIS.

◀ *Lake Kinneret is so-named because it is shaped like a "kinnor", or harp. It is 21 km long and 11 km wide and lies between the hills of Galilee and the Golan Heights. In winter, strong winds blow through the narrow valley, whipping up stormy waves on the lake.*

Although it is a small country, Israel has a wide range of climate and weather, from temperate to tropical. This is because it straddles the continents of Africa, Asia and Europe. The main differences occur between the northern part of the country and the Negev in the south.

The north has a typical Mediterranean climate, with plenty of sunshine – long, hot, dry summers and mild, wet winters. Summer lasts from mid-April to October. In the coastal areas, the heat can be oppressive and humid, with temperatures rising to over 30°C. Welcome afternoon sea breezes help to moderate the heat.

Winter lasts from November to February. Rain can be very heavy at times, with almost three-quarters of the annual rainfall expected during the months of December, January and February. Galilee is the wettest region, receiving over 1,000 mm of rain a year. But winters are generally mild, with plenty of intermittent sunshine.

Frost and snow are very rare, except in the hill regions. In 1993, for example, Jerusalem had only two days of snow.

The amount of rain in the semi-desert conditions of the Negev is very low, ranging from about 200 mm a year in the north to as little as 50 mm in Eilat. From time to time, there are thunderstorms in this region. These result in flash floods, and every year people drown as wadis become flooded

KEY FACTS

● Snow is rare outside the mountain regions. On the few days it snows in Jerusalem, excited schoolchildren, especially from the south, arrive by bus to make snowballs for the first time.
● In the rainy season, cloudbursts and violent storms can bring 100 mm of rainfall in just 24 hours.

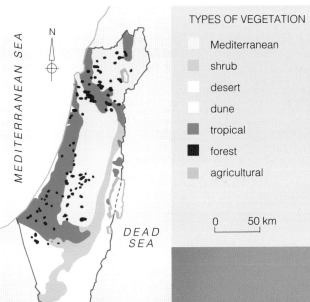

TYPES OF VEGETATION

- Mediterranean
- shrub
- desert
- dune
- tropical
- forest
- agricultural

0 50 km

MEDITERRANEAN SEA

N

DEAD SEA

RED SEA

within minutes. By contrast, summer temperatures in the Negev soar to more than 34°C in Beersheba and more than 40°C in Eilat.

The SHARAV (or Khamsin) is a scorching hot, dry desert wind which blows from the Arabian Desert from May to mid-June and from September to October. It lasts for two, three or even five days at a time. Tiny particles of sand penetrate everywhere and make life very uncomfortable!

► BEDOUIN *in the Negev. Tents provide shade during the day and help keep out the cold at night.*

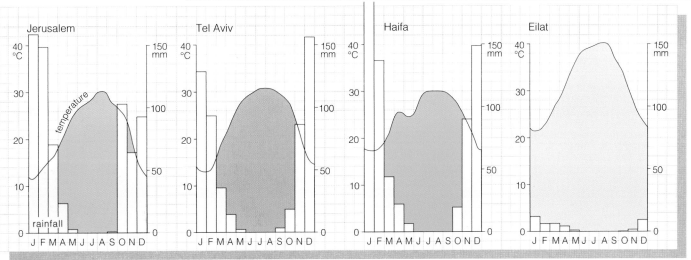

Jerusalem

Tel Aviv

Haifa

Eilat

Israel has very few natural resources. It relies on imported fuel for its power stations. Oil is bought from countries such as Egypt, and coal is imported from South Africa.

Scientific research into the development of solar energy, using heat from the sun, has produced an important alternative source of energy. Per head of population, Israel is the world's largest user of domestic solar-water heaters. By law, they are now installed in all new houses. A roof-top solar-water heater requires about three hours of

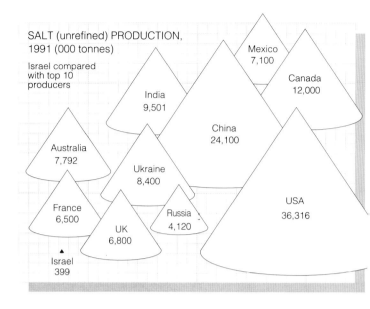

SALT (unrefined) PRODUCTION, 1991 (000 tonnes)

Israel compared with top 10 producers

Mexico 7,100
Canada 12,000
India 9,501
China 24,100
Australia 7,792
Ukraine 8,400
France 6,500
USA 36,316
Russia 4,120
UK 6,800
▲ Israel 399

sunshine a day to provide sufficient hot water for an average family of four. Even in winter, there is so much sunshine that only an occasional electric "booster" is needed.

In 1989, an experimental power plant was set up in the Negev to produce electricity and steam using oil shale deposits — clay rocks that contain residues of crude oil. They are the most abundant fossil energy resource discovered in Israel. The oil shales can produce 5 megawatts of electricity and 50 tonnes of steam per hour, and may be used for both industrial and domestic purposes. Further development of these resources is being planned.

The country's most valuable natural resources are phosphates: potash, magnesium, bromine and salt deposits from the Dead Sea. A significant amount is exported. These phosphates are valuable because of their use as chemical fertilizers.

Israel's only sources of fresh water are

◀ *Solar-powered street lights store energy from the sun to produce light at night-time. They are especially useful at isolated bus stops.*

▶ *Fresh water is a precious resource. Some regions have a better supply than others. The National Water Carrier brings water from the north to the dry south, using aqueducts, tunnels, dams, canals and pumping stations.*

KEY FACTS

● Between 1981 and 1995, Israel purchased 47 million tonnes of oil from Egypt for a total of about US$ 9 billion (at 1995 prices).
● Israel has a small copper mine near Eilat, but high costs mean that it has been closed since the mid-1980s.
● Thousands of people from all over the world come to Israel to seek treatment for skin diseases and ailments such as arthritis, as it is believed that mud and sulphur from the Dead Sea may provide a cure.

the River Jordan, Lake Kinneret, a few small rivers and natural springs, all of which are located in the north. The heaviest rains also fall in the north. In 1964, the National Water Carrier was built to make the best use of these limited resources. It brings water, through a system of canals and giant pipelines, from the north to the semi-arid regions in the south. This water is mainly used for irrigation and has helped to make parts of the desert fertile.

PHOSPHATE PRODUCTION, 1992 (000 tonnes)

top 10 producers

Tunisia 6,400

Germany 21,018

China 21,000

South Africa 3,080

Morocco 19,184

Brazil 2,459

Kazakhstan 6,680

USA 47,230

Jordan 4,296

Israel 3,596

POTASH PRODUCTION, 1993 (000 tonnes)

top 10 producers

UK 550

Spain 670

Belarus 1,900

Russia 2,600

Germany 2,800

France 900

Jordan 820

Israel 1,295

USA 1,500

Canada 6,840

POPULATION

Israel's fascinating multinational population is a melting pot of East and West. It includes both Jewish and non-Jewish citizens.

THE JEWISH POPULATION

When the state of Israel was founded in 1948, the Jewish population numbered 650,000. Today there are more than 4.6 million Jews, who have been drawn from almost every country in the world, with many differing cultures and religious customs. About 5.7 million people today live in Israel, the majority of whom are native-born.

There are two main Jewish groups. ASHKENAZI Jews are of Central and Eastern European origin, while SEPHARDI Jews come from North Africa, the Mediterranean area and Arabic-speaking countries.

Israel has welcomed many different groups of Jewish people into the country. Following the end of the Second World War, refugees arrived from several European

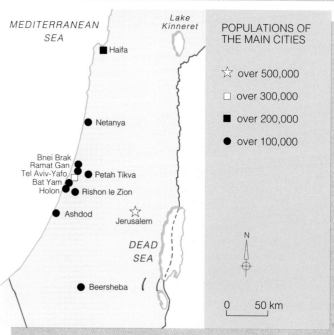

POPULATIONS OF THE MAIN CITIES

☆ over 500,000

☐ over 300,000

■ over 200,000

● over 100,000

MEDITERRANEAN SEA
Lake Kinneret
■ Haifa
● Netanya
Bnei Brak
Ramat Gan
Tel Aviv-Yafo
Bat Yam
Holon
● Petah Tikva
● Rishon le Zion
● Ashdod
☆ Jerusalem
DEAD SEA
● Beersheba

N

0   50 km

KEY FACTS

● Israel is a relatively young society. The average age is 26.6 years.

● In 1993, life expectancy was 75.3 years for men and 79.1 years for women – among the highest in the world.

● In 1994, the infant mortality rate was one of the lowest in the world – 7.5 per 1,000 births.

● Hebrew, Arabic and English are the official languages. Many others are spoken, including Yiddish, Russian and Amharic (Ethiopian).

● The Hebrew alphabet has 22 letters, plus 10 vowels that are written separately. Hebrew is written from right to left. "Shalom" means hello, goodbye and peace.

LARGEST JEWISH COMMUNITIES, 1991

Canada 360,000

UK 300,000

France 600,000

former USSR 1,449,117

USA 5,800,000

Israel 4,420,000

Brazil 100,000

Argentina 250,000

South Africa 114,000

Australia 100,000

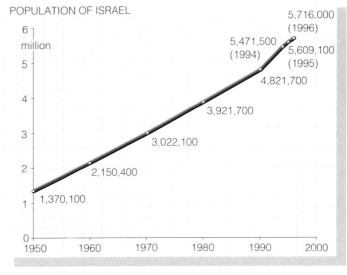

POPULATION OF ISRAEL

5,716,000 (1996)
5,471,500 (1994)
5,609,100 (1995)
4,821,700
3,921,700
3,022,100
2,150,400
1,370,100

▲ *In 1909, Tel Aviv was a tiny suburb of the ancient city of Yafo (Jaffa). Today, Yafo is part of the city area of Tel Aviv. The older buildings, with red tiled roofs, are now part of a vast urban sprawl.*

countries. The largest numbers came from Germany and Poland. After 1948, hundreds of thousands of Arabic-speaking Jews left their countries for Israel too. They came from places such as Afghanistan, Algeria, Morocco and Tunisia. Others came from as far away as Cochin in southern India. During the 1950s, almost the entire population of Jews from the Yemen (approximately 42,000) were flown to Israel in what became known as "Operation Magic Carpet". The Yemenite Jews spoke Hebrew, which helped them to integrate successfully into the modern state. In the 1980s, 44,600 Jews from Ethiopia were brought to Israel to escape from civil war and religious persecution. Most recently, since the fall of Communism in 1991, 627,000 Jews from the former Soviet Union have also settled in Israel.

Israel welcomes all newcomers, and works hard to settle them. The Jewish Agency,

with funds from international Jewish organizations and American grants and loans, has helped to provide immigrants with jobs, basic necessities and a place to live.

ISRAEL'S NON-JEWISH CITIZENS

Israel has 1,100,000 non-Jewish citizens – mainly Christian and Moslem Arabs and the DRUZE. The vast majority of the 835,000 Moslem Arabs are members of the Sunni sect, and make up 76% of the Arab population. They live in small towns and villages, mainly in the north of the country, with their own distinct culture and customs. There are also about 166,000 Christian Arabs, who belong to different religious groups. Most live in Nazareth, Haifa and Jerusalem.

Nearly 10% of the Moslem Arab population are Bedouin. They belong to about 30 different tribes in the southern Negev and Galilee. Today, the Bedouin are no longer entirely nomadic. They live in permanent settlements where jobs are more readily available and their children can receive an education. But about 40% still follow their traditional desert way of life, travelling by camel in search of grazing for

17

▲ *Greek Orthodox priests represent one of Israel's many Christian sects. The Orthodox calendar is different from that used by Catholics and Protestants. Christmas is celebrated on 7 January.*

◀ *A street sign in Hebrew, Arabic and English. Jerusalem's Armenian craftsmen are famous for producing such tiles.*

their flocks of sheep and goats. They live in black goat-skin tents, which can be easily folded and transported on the backs of their camels.

THE CITIES

Many new development towns such as Dimona, Yeruham and Kiryat Shemona were built in the 1950s to accommodate the growing population. Cheap apartment

POPULATION BY RELIGIOUS DENOMINATION (%)

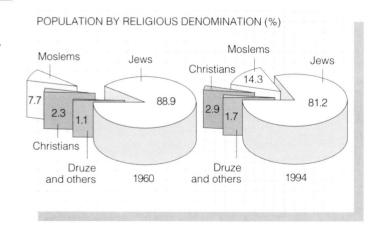

blocks were built as an emergency stop-gap to house Jewish immigrants, but many became overcrowded slums. Today, "Project Renewal" provides funds and volunteers, both Jewish and non-Jewish, from Europe and the USA to work in slum areas. They help to improve living conditions and to set up neighbourhood committees and community centres.

More than 90% of Israelis today live in cities. Many modern urban centres are built on ancient sites mentioned in the Bible, such as Jerusalem, Tiberias and Nazareth. Others began as agricultural villages and gradually grew into towns and cities. Because land is scarce, most city-dwellers live in apartment blocks. These normally have tiled floors and balconies. Modern villas with gardens are more numerous in suburbs and resort towns.

▼ *Passover is an important family festival. In Israel, it lasts for 7 days (although Jewish people abroad celebrate for 8 days). It begins with readings from the* HAGGADAH *which describe how the ancient Israelites passed from slavery in Egypt into freedom. Special food such as* MATZA *is eaten during the Passover festival.*

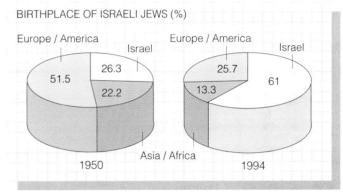

BIRTHPLACE OF ISRAELI JEWS (%)

1950: Europe / America 51.5, Israel 26.3, 22.2, Asia / Africa

1994: Europe / America 25.7, Israel 61, Asia / Africa 13.3

RURAL LIFE

About 10% of the population live in rural areas. Approximately 2.4% are members of the country's 270 KIBBUTZIM. A kibbutz is a CO-OPERATIVE community, mainly agricultural, whose members share ideals, work and responsibilities. They vote on important issues at regular meetings. Instead of wages, members receive a cash allowance, housing, food, clothing and medical care. Families can eat at home or in the communal dining hall. Children are cared for and educated collectively, so that their parents are free to work.

The MOSHAV is a collectively owned agricultural village. Unlike the kibbutz, its members live independent lives. Their produce is farmed and sold co-operatively. Israel has 450 moshavim, whose members make up 3.3% of the country's population.

▲ *Since 1984, about 44,000 Jews from Ethiopia have settled in Israel. These Ethiopian children go to school in Jerusalem.*

▶ *Arabs, like Jews, are family-minded. No meal is complete without friends and relations to share specially prepared dishes.*

DAILY LIFE

◀ *The kibbutz is a mainly agricultural community where people share all work and responsibilities. It runs its own schools and kindergartens. These nursery school teachers are using large trollies to take infants on their daily outing.*

WORK AND FAMILY LIFE

Israelis are hardworking people. Most work for five and a half days a week, although there is a growing trend towards a five-day week. People in offices work an eight-hour day, without a break, from 7.30 am to 3.30 pm. Banks, offices, schools and Jewish shops close at noon on Friday and reopen on Sunday morning. This is because the Jewish Sabbath begins at sunset on Friday and ends on Saturday evening. There is no public transport on Saturdays, except in Haifa, which has a large Arab population. Moslem shops are closed on Fridays and Christian shops on Sundays.

On Friday evenings, Jewish families and friends get together to enjoy the Sabbath meal. Before the Sabbath begins, religious Jews pray at the synagogue or at the Western Wall (the remains of the ancient temple in Jerusalem). Non-religious people may enjoy sport and leisure activities instead.

Family celebrations are important. They include BAR-MITZVAHS and other festivals.

Israeli Arabs, both Christian and Moslem, live in traditional extended families, often with two or three generations gathered under one roof. They have their own culture and customs. For example, a wedding is celebrated by holding a special party every day for several days before the marriage ceremony.

RELIGION

Religious freedom is granted to the entire population. Each religion has the right to practise its faith and appoint its own leaders. Jerusalem is the centre of three great religions: Judaism, Christianity and Islam. Their most sacred holy places in Jerusalem are near each other within the old walled city and are protected by law.

ORTHODOX (religious) Jews pray at the Western Wall. Nearby is the Dome of the

DAILY LIFE

Rock with its magnificent gold dome. It is a monument to the Prophet Mohammed. On Fridays, their holy day, thousands of Moslems worship at the El Aksa Mosque. Christians pray at the Church of the Holy Sepulchre, which contains the tomb of Jesus.

HEALTH

The National Health Service is based on medical services provided by insurance schemes. Jerusalem's Hadassah hospital is the largest in the Middle East. It treats more than 60,000 patients a year, regardless of religion or nationality.

Israel's emergency service, "Magen David Adom", provides ambulances, first-aid stations and a blood donor programme. Around 4,500 volunteers are involved in the various branches.

There are also approximately 900 mother and child health centres in Israel, which are run by local or national authorities.

MAJOR FESTIVALS AND HOLIDAYS

Both the Jewish and Moslem calendars are based on the moon, not the sun, so dates of festivals vary each year. In 1997, the major festivals are:

JEWISH FESTIVALS

23 March 1997	PURIM (commemorates the story of Queen Esther)
22–29 April 1997	PASSOVER (commemorates the exodus of the Israelites from Egypt)
11 June 1997	SHAVU'OT (commemorates the giving of the Law to Moses)
2–3 October 1997	ROSH HASHANA (New Year 5758)
11 October 1997	YOM KIPPUR (Day of Atonement)
26 October 1997	SUKKOT (Feast of the Tabernacles)
24–31 December 1997	HANUKKAH (Festival of Lights)

NATIONAL HOLIDAYS

4 May 1997	Holocaust Martyrs' and Heroes' Remembrance Day
11 May 1997	Remembrance Day for the Fallen of Israel's Wars
12 May 1997	Independence Day
4 June 1997	Jerusalem Day

MOSLEM FESTIVALS

9–12 February 1997	ID AL-FITR (the end of Ramadan)
9–22 April 1997	ID AL-ADHA (related to the Haj, or pilgrimage to Mecca)
9 May 1997	1 MUHARRAM (New Year 1418)
18 July 1997	PROPHET MOHAMMED'S BIRTHDAY

CHRISTIAN FESTIVALS

31 March 1997	EASTER SUNDAY (Catholic and Protestant)
27 April 1997	EASTER SUNDAY (Orthodox)
25 December 1997	CHRISTMAS DAY (Catholic and Protestant)
[7 January 1998	CHRISTMAS DAY (Orthodox)]

◀ *At the age of 13, a Jewish boy celebrates his bar-mitzvah and, according to tradition, becomes an adult. During the ceremony, he reads a passage from the TORAH scroll (Jewish scripture). The bar-mitzvah boy here wears a prayer shawl and skull cap.*

▶ *There are almost 800,000 Moslem Arabs in Israel, most of whom are members of the Sunni sect. Moslems turn in the direction of their holy city of Mecca to say their prayers, which they do 5 times every day. These Arabs are praying at the El Aksa Mosque in Jerusalem.*

EDUCATION

Both religious and secular (non-religious) education have a high priority in Israel. The country spends 6% of its GROSS NATIONAL PRODUCT (GNP) on education, compared with 5.3% in the UK.

There are three different types of Jewish schools: 69% of children attend state schools, 21% attend state religious schools and 10% attend independent religious schools.

State education, including kindergarten for five year-olds, is compulsory up to 16 years of age and free between the ages of five and 18. Up to the age of 13 years, children go to school from 8 am till 1 pm. High-school pupils (aged 14 years and older) stay till 2 pm. Before this, almost all three and four year-olds have some kind of pre-school education, which is not free.

KEY FACTS

● Women make up 40% of the workforce, and 68% of these are mothers with children under the age of 15.
● In Israel, there are 466 doctors for every 100,000 people.
● Pre-school attendance is the highest in the world. 97% of 3 and 4 year-olds go to a nursery school or play group.
● 13 Hebrew newspapers and 11 foreign language newspapers are printed daily. The *Jerusalem Post* is the only English daily newspaper.
● There are 2 television channels as well as cable television. Programmes are broadcast in Hebrew, Arabic and several other languages.

◀ *Israeli schoolchildren start first grade at 6 years old. Among other subjects, pupils study Jewish history, the Hebrew Bible and foreign languages, including Arabic (although this is not compulsory). Local geography is very popular and children often go on field trips with their teachers.*

EDUCATIONAL SYSTEM – NUMBER OF STUDENTS (000s)

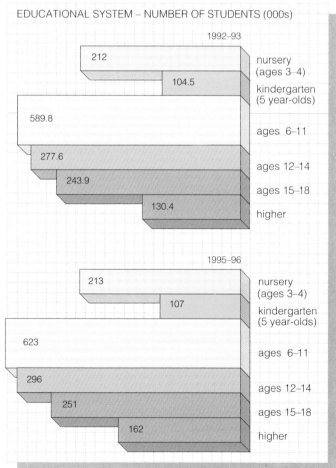

1992–93

212	nursery (ages 3–4)
104.5	kindergarten (5 year-olds)
589.8	ages 6–11
277.6	ages 12–14
243.9	ages 15–18
130.4	higher

1995–96

213	nursery (ages 3–4)
107	kindergarten (5 year-olds)
623	ages 6–11
296	ages 12–14
251	ages 15–18
162	higher

STUDENTS' FIELDS OF STUDY, 1993–94 (%)
(higher education)

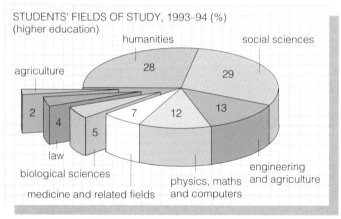

humanities 28
social sciences 29
agriculture 2
4
5
7
12
13
law
biological sciences
medicine and related fields
physics, maths and computers
engineering and agriculture

State religious schools emphasize Jewish studies and religious observance. Independent Torah schools are for ULTRA-ORTHODOX children. Boys and girls are taught in separate buildings.

Arab and Druze children go to Arabic-language schools, where they learn Hebrew as well as the history and culture of their own faiths. There are also a number of Jewish, Christian and Moslem private schools.

Israel has eight universities, including the Open University of Israel, and a network of vocational training schools. About 35% of young people who are of an age to go to university are students, compared with 20% in the UK and 58% in the USA. But the average age of students is higher in Israel because of the need to carry out compulsory military service between 18 and 21 years of age. In the WEST BANK and Gaza, there are five teacher-training colleges and five universities.

The ULPAN system for adults and children provides free intensive education programmes for new immigrants. They are taught Hebrew, Jewish history, customs and traditions.

SPORT

League soccer and basketball are the most popular sports in Israel. Other sports include tennis, swimming, wind-surfing, snorkelling and scuba-diving. Sports stadia and training facilities are provided by regional and local authorities.

Jewish athletes from around the world compete in the Maccabiah Games which are held in Israel every four years. The games are known as the "Jewish Olympics".

▼ *League basketball is organized at local, regional and national levels. Matches always attract large, enthusiastic audiences.*

RULE AND LAW

◀ *The Menorah, a seven-branched candelabrum, is the official emblem of the state of Israel. This giant Menorah, a gift from the UK, stands near the Knesset building in Jerusalem. Its carvings portray the history of the Jewish people.*

Israel is a parliamentary democracy. The Knesset, or parliament, is elected every four years. It has 120 members, including Arab and Druze representatives. The head of state is the President, who is elected by members of the Knesset and serves for a period of five years.

Everyone over the age of 18 has the vote. Voters choose both a candidate for Prime Minister and the political party they want to represent them. The Prime Minister is head of the government. There are two main parties, Labour and Likud (conservative). The Likud party was elected in 1996, but without a clear majority. It depends on the support of smaller, mainly religious, parties to maintain itself in power.

Military service in the Israel Defence Force (IDF), which includes the army, navy and airforce, is compulsory for all eligible, medically fit men and women at the age of 18. Men serve for three years, and women for two. After this, men serve part-time in

the Army Reserves until they reach 45 years of age and in the Civil Defence until they are 55 years old. Married women, ultra-Orthodox Jews (who devote their lives to religious studies) and non-Jews are exempt from military service.

Israel depends upon the IDF to protect its borders, as many of the country's Arab neighbours refuse to recognise its existence. Border clashes and terrorist attacks are commonplace. For example, after a war in 1967, Israel took over the Golan Heights

Diagram:

THE PRESIDENT
elected by the Knesset
every 5 years

THE KNESSET
120 members
elected every
4 years

legislative

THE GOVERNMENT
(executive)

THE PRIME MINISTER

MINISTRIES

THE SPEAKER

COMMITTEES

STATE COMPTROLLER

THE JUDICIARY

THE ATTORNEY-GENERAL

COURTS OF LAW

LOCAL COUNCILS

MAYORS

COUNCIL HEADS

THE ELECTORATE

area from Syria, and today there are still disputes about where the border between the two countries should lie.

In 1994, the Palestinian National Authority (PNA) was granted control in Gaza and Jericho. In 1995, it also gained control of parts of the West Bank where 70% of the area's Arab population live, including six major towns. The PNA opposes any further Jewish settlements in these areas. The status of Hebron is still under negotiation.

A change of government in Israel in 1996 slowed down the peace process. A major obstacle to peace in the region is that both Jewish and Moslem extremists continue to reject the idea of reaching an agreement.

Women soldiers serve in most branches of the Israel Defence Force, but do not go into battle.

KEY FACTS

● Israel's flag is based on the design of a Jewish prayer shawl with a blue Star of David.
● Although Arabs are exempted from the IDF, there are many Bedouin volunteers, who are famous for their tracking and scouting skills.
● The growth of Jewish Orthodox extremism in Jerusalem has led to violent clashes with secular Jews over the use of private vehicles on the Sabbath. Police have to control the disturbances.

The IDF and the Palestine police force now have joint patrols in the West Bank and Gaza.

FOOD AND FARMING

Irrigation has revolutionized agriculture in Israel. Since 1948, the total area under cultivation has more than doubled to 440,000 hectares, while irrigated land has increased eight-fold to about 240,000 hectares. Israel's agricultural success has been achieved by close co-operation between farmers and agricultural scientists. The old, costly and wasteful irrigation method of using water-sprinklers has been replaced by a computerized drip system. Perforated plastic tubing allows each plant to be supplied with nutrients and water drip by drip. This technique has turned thousands of hectares of desert into arable land. In addition, new strains of crops have been developed which can tolerate the desert climate and give improved yields. The kibbutz and moshav farming communities supply the home market with fruit, vegetables, dairy products and poultry, as well as trout, carp and salmon, which are bred in fish farms.

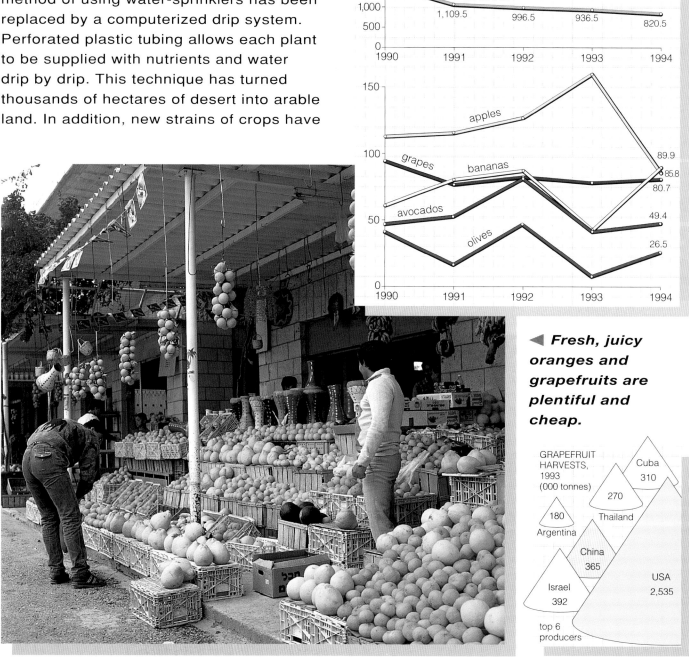

HARVESTS (000 tonnes)

citrus fruit
1,506.1
1,109.5
996.5
936.5
820.5
1990 1991 1992 1993 1994

apples 89.9
grapes 85.8
bananas 80.7
avocados 49.4
olives 26.5
1990 1991 1992 1993 1994

◀ *Fresh, juicy oranges and grapefruits are plentiful and cheap.*

GRAPEFRUIT HARVESTS, 1993 (000 tonnes)

Cuba 310
Thailand 270
Argentina 180
China 365
Israel 392
USA 2,535

top 6 producers

Farming practices are changing, but some Israeli Arab farmers still use traditional methods such as TERRACING hillsides. They grow grapes and olives in their smallholdings, and herd sheep for meat and wool.

Although pasture land for cows is scarce, milk production is high for a small country.

In 1993, the average dairy cow produced 9,500 kg of milk. The most successful dairy producer was kibbutz Negba, where the average output per cow reached 11,845 kg.

Israel's chief agricultural imports are grain, oil seeds, meat, coffee, cocoa and sugar. Its most successful agricultural

◄ *Early-morning shoppers at this market stall like to buy their bread piping hot straight from the ovens. Large, flat Iraqi bread is baked on the sides of the oven. Round bagels (often sprinkled with sesame and poppy seeds) are firm favourites.*

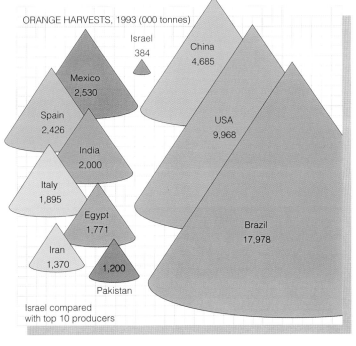

ORANGE HARVESTS, 1993 (000 tonnes)

Israel 384
China 4,685
Mexico 2,530
Spain 2,426
USA 9,968
India 2,000
Italy 1,895
Egypt 1,771
Brazil 17,978
Iran 1,370
1,200 Pakistan

Israel compared with top 10 producers

KEY FACTS

● Ancient Jewish laws require all fields to lie fallow every 7th year.
● Between 1985 and 1994, individual consumption of fresh vegetables rose by 32%, from 134 kg to 177 kg a year.
● The English language does not have an equivalent of the French saying "Bon appetit" (good appetite). The Israelis say "Be'tayavon", which means the same.
● Israelis have an addiction to chewing "garinim" – roasted and salted sunflower, pumpkin and watermelon seeds. They are eaten, like bags of crisps, anywhere, anytime.

◀ **Felafel stalls are part of the Israeli way of life. A felafel is filled with fried chick peas and items such as pickles, olives, salads and spicy sauces. It is important not to over-fill it. Carried in a napkin, it can be eaten and enjoyed anywhere.**

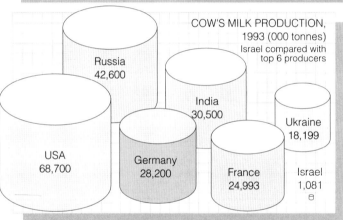

COW'S MILK PRODUCTION, 1993 (000 tonnes)
Israel compared with top 6 producers

Russia 42,600
India 30,500
Ukraine 18,199
USA 68,700
Germany 28,200
France 24,993
Israel 1,081

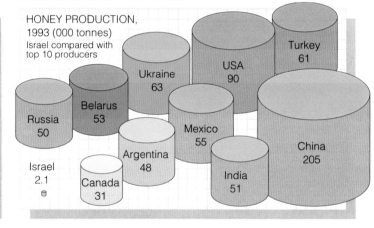

HONEY PRODUCTION, 1993 (000 tonnes)
Israel compared with top 10 producers

Turkey 61
USA 90
Ukraine 63
Belarus 53
Russia 50
Mexico 55
China 205
Israel 2.1
Argentina 48
Canada 31
India 51

exports include citrus fruits, melons, tomatoes, cucumbers and avocados.

The unique blend of East and West in the country has produced a great variety of Jewish ethnic cooking traditions, ranging from bourekas (puff pastries filled with cheese, from the Middle East) to borscht (a thick beetroot soup, from Eastern Europe). Bread comes in every shape and size. Freshly baked plaited CHALOT are bought on Fridays for the Sabbath meal. Soft, flat Arab pitta bread is well known. Its hollow "pocket" is filled with fried chick peas, pickles, salad and a spicy sauce. This is felafel, the country's most famous snack

food. There is an entire street of felafel stalls in Tel Aviv.

Most Jewish restaurants and all official public eating places serve KOSHER food, prepared according to ancient Jewish dietary laws. These forbid the eating of certain foods, such as all products derived from pigs, and shellfish. Meat and dairy foods may not be eaten together. Not all Israelis observe these rules. Moslems have their own dietary rules, which also forbid the eating of pork and similar products.

Local produce and imported American and European foods line the shelves of modern air-conditioned supermarkets.

Domestic goods include many kinds of delicious yoghurts and white cheeses made from sheep, goat and cow's milk. Open-air markets attract shoppers who like to browse among mountains of fruit and vegetables, which are picked and delivered daily. There are also stalls specializing in roasted nuts and seeds, dried fruit and a great range of aromatic herbs and spices. Street kiosks sell fresh orange, grapefruit, carrot and kiwi-fruit juice, squeezed while you wait.

Every Jewish festival is celebrated with its own special food. Apples and honey are symbolic of a sweet New Year, while doughnuts and potato LATKES are eaten at Hanukkah and HAMENTASHEN at Purim. During the seven days of Passover, ordinary bread and flour products are replaced by matza and matza meal. Matzabrie (fried matza), coconut pyramid cakes and kneidle (soup dumplings) are all firm favourites.

Arab specialities include puff pastries called kunafa and sambusak. Kunafa has a sweet filling, while sambusak may be filled with either sweet or savoury items.

▼ *The lakeside restaurant at kibbutz Ein Gev specializes in serving St Peter's fish (also called "amnon"), which is caught in Lake Kinneret.*

◀ *Israelis refer to Eilat as "sof olam" – the end of the world! Thousands of tourists enjoy the year-round sunshine at this resort on the Red Sea. Outdoor activities include sailing, scuba-diving and snorkelling among rare tropical fish and corals.*

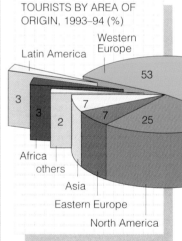

TOURISTS BY AREA OF ORIGIN, 1993–94 (%)

Latin America

Western Europe

53

3

3

7

2

7

25

Africa
others

Asia

Eastern Europe

North America

EXPORT MARKETS AND DEVELOPMENTS

During the first half of the 1990s, Israel's economy, with the help of aid from the USA and international Jewish organizations, had a high growth rate compared to those in the West. This economic achievement has attracted foreign investment to the value of US$ 1 billion.

Israel has a small economy and a limited domestic market. Economic growth depends on finding new export markets. In the past, the political situation prevented trade with most of Israel's neighbours. Since the start of the new round of peace talks, which began in 1994, trade agreements have been signed with Egypt, Jordan, Tunisia and Morocco. In addition to Western markets, Israel also has good trade links with China, India and South Korea. Japan has opened

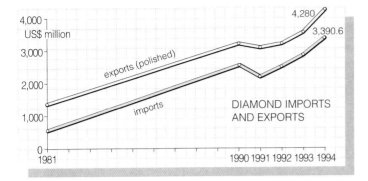

DIAMOND IMPORTS AND EXPORTS

4,000 US$ million
3,000
exports (polished) — 4,280
3,390.6
2,000
imports
1,000
0
1981 1990 1991 1992 1993 1994

DESTINATION OF DIAMOND EXPORTS, 1994 (%)

Switzerland
USA 45
3
8
10
17
17
others
Belgium
Hong Kong
Japan

► *Polished diamonds are a key export. Here, the stones are examined for imperfections. It takes great skill to cut them correctly.*

an official trade office in Tel Aviv too.

Israel has a well-trained, highly skilled workforce, but lacks most basic raw materials. Industry, therefore, concentrates on manufactured products and scientific and technological development. Israel allocates 10% of its national spending to scientific research. Developments in agricultural techniques and technology, fine chemicals, computer hardware and software, and medical electronics have reached international standards. Israel has 90% of the world market in some areas of electro-optics, and the USA buys almost a third of its surgical lasers from Israel.

THE DIAMOND INDUSTRY

Israel is the world's leading exporter of polished diamonds. The industry was set up in the 1950s by a group of skilled Belgian and Dutch Jewish refugees. Exports now exceed US$ 4 billion a year. The Diamond

Exchange in Ramat Gan, near Tel Aviv, is the centre of the industry. Not all diamonds are made into jewellery. Some of the rough, uncut stones, which are imported from Asia and Africa, are used in drilling and cutting machines.

TOURISM

Because of Israel's climate, tourists visit the country all year round. The tourist industry is worth about US$ 1 billion annually and plays a vital role in Israel's economy. More than 2 million tourists arrive every year. Holiday-makers flock to resort hotels. International and domestic flights take visitors direct to Eilat for water-sports and winter sunshine. Archaeological sites and excavations are another important attraction. Youth hostels are crowded with European backpackers and many young people join kibbutz volunteer programmes. Among the tourists are around 300,000 pilgrims who join tours of the Holy Land which are specially organized to include sacred Christian sites.

A large number of tourists are Jewish people from abroad. They visit relatives, take courses at a religious centre or university, celebrate Jewish festivals, or visit Yad Vashem in Jerusalem, the official memorial to the 6 million Jews killed in the Nazi Holocaust of the Second World War.

CONSTRUCTION

In the first 25 years of the new state, residential building accounted for 84% of the total construction output. This percentage is continually fluctuating to meet the needs of the growing population

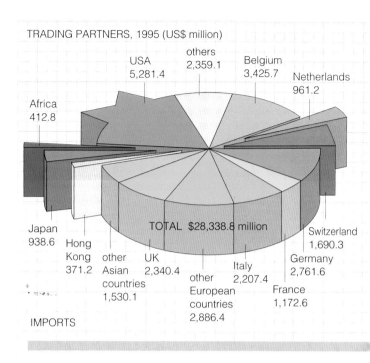

TRADING PARTNERS, 1995 (US$ million)

others 2,359.1
USA 5,281.4
Belgium 3,425.7
Netherlands 961.2
Africa 412.8
TOTAL $28,338.8 million
Switzerland 1,690.3
Japan 938.6
Hong Kong 371.2
other Asian countries 1,530.1
UK 2,340.4
Italy 2,207.4
Germany 2,761.6
other European countries 2,886.4
France 1,172.6
IMPORTS

▼ *The Dead Sea Works company uses modern, computerized techniques to extract phosphates: potash, magnesium, bromine and salt. Exports are worth US$ 500 million a year.*

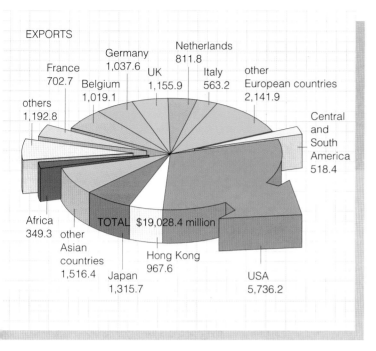

EXPORTS

France 702.7
Germany 1,037.6
Belgium 1,019.1
Netherlands 811.8
UK 1,155.9
Italy 563.2
other European countries 2,141.9
others 1,192.8
Central and South America 518.4
Africa 349.3
other Asian countries 1,516.4
Japan 1,315.7
Hong Kong 967.6
USA 5,736.2

TOTAL $19,028.4 million

▶ *The Weizmann Institute in Rehovot is an important science research centre. Scientists help industry by developing a wide variety of electronic and high-tech equipment for export.*

KEY FACTS

● The Israeli workforce is divided into 33% involved in industry, agriculture and construction, 6% in transport and communications and 61% in public and commercial services.
● Polished diamonds from Israel account for 35% of those used in new jewellery throughout the world.
● On average, visitors spend 17.5 nights in Israel, putting the country in the top 5 tourist destinations measured by length of stay.
● Haifa Technion University, where farmers and scientists work together, has the largest agricultural engineering faculty in the world.

and new immigrants. A total of 83,000 new apartments were built in 1991, compared with 43,000 in 1992 and 33,600 in 1993.

HISTADRUT

The majority of Israel's labour force, including both Jews and Arabs, belong to the Histadrut – the General Federation of Labour. Its members come from all branches of the economy, from dock-workers to bank managers. The Histadrut provides jobs as well as representing its members. Until recently, it operated Israel's largest health insurance scheme, and it continues to provide educational and welfare services for its members.

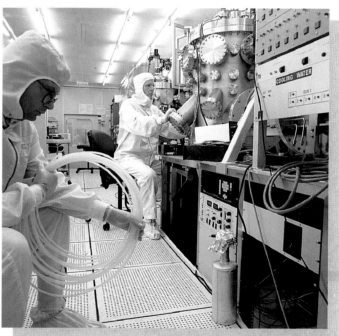

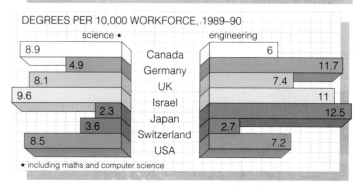

DEGREES PER 10,000 WORKFORCE, 1989–90

	science ★	engineering
Canada	8.9	6
Germany	4.9	11.7
UK	8.1	7.4
Israel	9.6	11
Japan	2.3	12.5
Switzerland	3.6	2.7
USA	8.5	7.2

★ including maths and computer science

TRANSPORT

Israel has a modernized road network system which links the country's major business, cultural and holiday centres. Road signs are in Hebrew, English and Arabic. Rising prosperity has enabled more people to buy cars. In 1994, there were more than 1,470,000 private cars on the roads and Israel now has one of the most congested road systems in the world. There are about 500 fatal road accidents every year, and the death toll continues to rise. Experts believe that, in spite of vehicle inspections, they may be caused by a high percentage of inexperienced teenagers driving unroadworthy, second-hand cars, as well as too many scooters and motor-cycles. A total of 58,323 motor-cycles were purchased in 1994 alone.

One of the most popular means of transport in Israel is travelling by bus. The Egged Bus Company is a co-operative owned by its drivers. It is the third largest bus company in the world in terms of passengers carried, with a turnover of US$ 342 million in 1991. It has a fleet of 4,000 air-conditioned buses which operate all urban and intercity services, except in Tel Aviv, where another company operates. Except in Haifa, buses do not run between dusk on Friday and dusk on Saturday.

The SHERUT TAXI is special to Israel. It is a shared taxi which holds up to seven passengers, operating a direct service between its own fixed stations. There is a set price, which is a little more than the

▼ *Bus stations are always crowded because the service is so popular. Some local buses run till midnight. Senior citizens can travel for half price.*

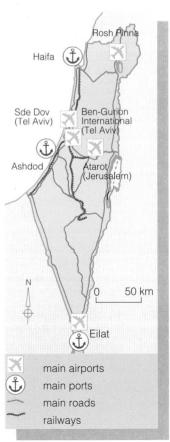

✈	main airports
⚓	main ports
〰	main roads
	railways

TRANSPORT

▲ *Tel Aviv's modern station caters for a growing number of rail passengers. Two new commuter stations are used for travel between the city and the suburbs.*

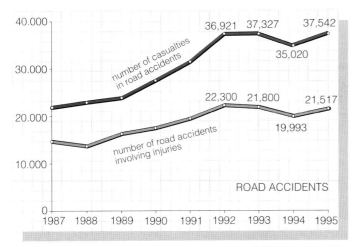

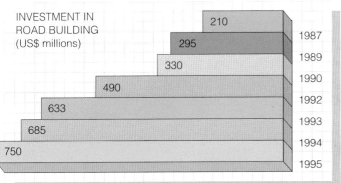

bus fare for the same journey.

Israel's international airline is El Al. In 1993, its turnover was US$ 947.1 million. In the same year, it carried 2,154,000 passengers into and out of Israel. The company is also a major cargo transporter for Israel's agricultural and industrial exports.

Ben-Gurion International Airport in Tel Aviv handled 6.8 million passengers in 1995. This was 15% more than the 1994 total. A modern new terminal was opened in 1994 which has improved passenger services. Arkia, Israel's domestic airline, links the major cities.

Railway passenger services are limited and unprofitable. There are rail links between Jerusalem, Tel Aviv, Haifa and Nahariya. However, trains have recently become more of an accepted method of

▼ *Good road links have brought benefits even to remote communities. But in spite of 6-lane motorways serving the ports and industrial and business districts, traffic congestion has become a major problem.*

passenger transport. This is due to the development of new commuter lines as a welcome alternative to road delays. A major new modern rail expansion scheme, "Project Railway 2000", which will include Israel's first underground train, is being planned. Freight train services operate in the south, serving Ashdod and the mineral quarries near Dimona.

The modern deep-water ports of Haifa, Eilat and Ashdod serve international shipping. Haifa is one of the largest container ports in the Mediterranean, as well as a passenger terminal.

▼ *Haifa is a modern port used by luxury liners, tankers and cargo boats. Here, oranges are being loaded for shipment to Europe.*

KEY FACTS

● In 1996, the government decided to take tough measures to reduce road accidents by increasing traffic fines. Failure to stop at traffic lights will cost a driver US$ 625 instead of US$ 125. A repeat offence will cost US$ 940 instead of US$ 170.

● In 1995, the USA had 30 vehicles per km of road, Spain 40, Japan 52 and Germany 59. Israel had 100: the world's highest figure.

● Traffic laws are strict. Seat belts are compulsory. Speed limits are 90 kph on motorways and 50–70 kph in urban areas.

● The journey from Tel Aviv to Jerusalem takes 1 hour, 40 minutes by train, winding through the Sorek valley, and costs US$ 4.20. The same journey by Sherut taxi takes 45 minutes and costs US$ 4.60.

THE ENVIRONMENT

◀ *Tree planting helps to prevent soil erosion and create recreation areas. These children are planting saplings to celebrate Tu B'Shevat – Israel's Arbor Day. Millions of trees are planted every year in Israel.*

Planting trees to help protect the soil from erosion became a national priority after 1948. Since then, 200 million trees have been planted all over the country. Four million trees are planted every year. Tu B'Shevat, the 15th day of the Jewish month of Shevat, is Israel's Arbor Day. It is celebrated by planting trees, which are often used to mark birthdays and special events.

Several nature conservation groups, appointed by the government, work closely together. For example, the Society for the Protection of Nature operates 24 field schools, providing intensive educational programmes on nature protection and conservation.

More than 4,000 square kilometres of land have been set aside for Israel's 280 nature reserves. The Hula lake area was once malarial swamp and marshland. Between 1951 and 1957, a massive

drainage project was begun here to create new farming land, but 310 hectares were left untouched. In 1964, this area was officially declared Israel's first wildlife nature reserve.

Because Israel lies at the crossroads of three continents, plant and animal life is especially rich. Creatures such as the ibex, leopard and vulture are protected species. The country has more than 2,800 different types of plants and about 380 different species of birds. Every year, hundreds of thousands of migrating birds pass through Israel. Places like the Hula reserve provide magnificent opportunities for serious bird-watching.

Hai-Bar, which means "wildlife", was established in the mid-1960s to reintroduce animals that once lived in Israel. So far the white oryx, Asiatic wild ass, addax antelope and a local species of ostrich have been rescued from near extinction and

▲ *The ibex lives in the mountainous regions of the Negev. In spite of its great size and heavy horns, it is surprisingly nimble and sure-footed.*

successfully reintroduced into the wild. Similarly, Neot Kedumim is a botanical reserve which collects and conserves plants mentioned in the Bible.

Pollution in Israel comes from highly industrialized urban areas, 70% of which are concentrated along the narrow Mediterranean coastal strip. Israel belongs to the Mediterranean Action Plan –

Nahal Ayoun
Tel Dan
Nahal Hermon
Ein Afeq
Hula
Gamla
Nahal Mearot
Soreq Cave
Ein Gedi
DEAD SEA
MAIN NATURE RESERVES
Eilat Coral Beach Reserve
RED SEA
MEDITERRANEAN SEA
N
0   50 km

◀ *The Ein Gedi Nature Reserve is a desert oasis near the Dead Sea. Waterfalls and streams produce lush vegetation which attracts the leopard, the ibex and the hyrax (rock-rabbit).*

a non-political organization involved in programmes to clean up beaches and the water. Water polluted by the intensive use of chemical fertilizers and pesticides has become a critical problem. One high priority is to treat waste water so that it can be used for irrigation purposes. Pollutant emissions caused by increased traffic are being combated by introducing cheaper lead-free petrol. Other measures include the government's stipulation in 1995 that diesel fuel should contain no more than 0.2% sulphur – down from 0.3%.

KEY FACTS

● Wherever schoolchildren plant trees, they return every year to record the development of their saplings.
● Some forests are named after famous people, such as Queen Elizabeth II and the late US President J. F. Kennedy.
● Israel's worst forest fire occurred on 2 July 1995 near Jerusalem. About 2 million trees were destroyed.
● 60% of Eilat's fresh water requirements are provided by desalination, a process of extracting salt from sea and brackish water.

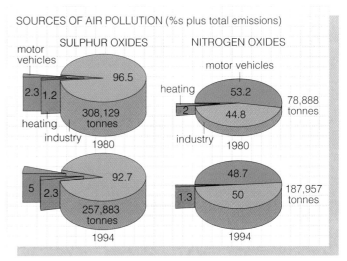

SOURCES OF AIR POLLUTION (%s plus total emissions)

SULPHUR OXIDES
motor vehicles
2.3 1.2 96.5
heating
industry
308,129 tonnes
1980

5 2.3 92.7
257,883 tonnes
1994

NITROGEN OXIDES
motor vehicles
heating
2 53.2 44.8
industry
78,888 tonnes
1980

1.3 48.7 50
187,957 tonnes
1994

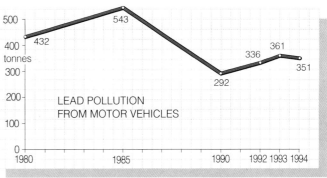

LEAD POLLUTION FROM MOTOR VEHICLES

500 — 543
432
400
tonnes   336 361
300   292   351
200
100
0
1980   1985   1990   1992 1993 1994

Peace is vital for Israel and its neighbours. Since 1948, they have fought five wars. The hostility is rooted in the strong and ancient claims of two peoples to a small area of land. An acceptable solution to the Arab–Israeli conflict has still to be agreed. Meanwhile, the cost in human life is high and taxes, to pay for defence, are a heavy burden.

Egypt was the first Middle Eastern country to sign a peace treaty with Israel. As a result, in 1979 Prime Minister Begin of Israel and President Sadat of Egypt were jointly awarded the Nobel Peace Prize. Sadat was assassinated in 1981. In July 1994, King Hussein of Jordan and Prime Minister Rabin of Israel signed a peace accord. A year later, Rabin was assassinated by a right-wing Jewish student. Many world leaders attended his funeral, including King Hussein.

In 1994, a new round of Middle East peace talks began. These are diplomatic discussions aimed at reaching agreement between Israel, Palestine and all the neighbouring Arab states. Co-operation and commitment are an important aspect of peace. Joint projects with Jordan and Egypt, such as sharing water and energy resources, are being planned within the framework of the peace talks. The creation of a Mediterranean and Middle East electricity grid, for example, would benefit a population of some 300 million people.

Many moderate Arabs and Jews support the peace process, because of its advantages for everyone in the Middle East. But the influence of religious and nationalist extremists on both sides has to be curtailed if the peace process is to succeed.

◀ *On 4 November 1995, Prime Minister Yitzhak Rabin was assassinated at a peace rally in Jerusalem. World leaders and old enemies came to Israel to pay their respects at his funeral.*

▼ *On 4 September 1996, Prime Minister Binyamin Netanyahu and Yassir Arafat, the leader of the PNA, met for the first time, to restore confidence in the peace process.*

KEY FACTS

- Israel's national anthem is called "Hatikva", which means "The Hope".
- In 1996, the first ever scheduled El Al flight from Ben-Gurion Airport to Amman, the capital of Jordan, took place.
- There are a number of government initiatives for Israeli–Arab understanding. Givat Haviva and Neve Shalom/Wahat al-Salam are 2 institutions which teach peaceful co-existence to both adults and children.

FURTHER INFORMATION

● THE EMBASSY OF ISRAEL
2 Palace Green, London W8 4QB
Provides general information on Israel.

● BIPAC (BRITAIN ISRAEL PUBLIC AFFAIRS CENTRE)
21–22 Great Sutton Street, London EC1V 0DN
Issues a monthly bulletin on political and economic affairs in Israel.

● ISRAEL GOVERNMENT TOURIST OFFICE
18 Great Marlborough Street, London W1V 1AF
Provides information such as maps and leaflets.

● KIBBUTZ REPRESENTATIVES
1a Accommodation Road, London NW11 8ED
Provides an information pack on kibbutzim.

BOOKS ABOUT ISRAEL
Inside Israel, Ian James, Franklin Watts 1990 (age 9–13)
Israel, Mike Rogoff, Macmillan 1990 (age 9–13)
Jerusalem, Saviour Pirotta, Evans 1993 (age 9–13)
What Do We Know about Judaism? Doreen Fine, Macdonald Young Books 1995 (age 9–13)

GLOSSARY

ASHKENAZI
A term used to describe Jewish people from Central and Eastern Europe.

BAR-MITZVAH
The religious celebration held for a Jewish boy at the age of 13 when, according to tradition, he becomes an adult.

BEDOUIN
A tribal people who live in the Negev and Galilee. They make up 10% of Israel's Moslem Arab population. Only 40% still live a wholly nomadic life.

CHALAH (plural CHALOT)
The Hebrew word for a plaited loaf of bread. Two are eaten during the Sabbath meal.

CO-OPERATIVE
An association of farmers or other groups who pool their resources, work together and share the profits.

DRUZE
A group of people whose religion contains elements of the Moslem faith, but with significant variations. About 95,000 live in northern Israel.

GROSS NATIONAL PRODUCT
The total value of all the goods and services produced by a country in a year.

HAGGADAH
The Haggadah tells the story of the exodus of the Israelites from Egypt more than 3,000 years ago. It is read on the first night of the Passover festival.

HAMANTASHEN
A three-cornered shaped pastry with a sweet filling which is eaten during the festival of Purim.

HOLOCAUST
The murder of 6 million Jews during the Second World War by the Nazi regime in Germany.

KIBBUTZ (plural KIBBUTZIM)
A co-operative farming community where people share ideals, responsibilities and work. Instead of wages, the kibbutz provides its members with housing, education and food.

KOSHER
Jewish dietary laws. They forbid the eating of all products derived from pigs and of shellfish, and stipulate that meat and dairy products should not be prepared or eaten together.

LATKE
A fried potato cake eaten during the Hanukkah festival.

MATZA
Flat, unleavened bread (made without yeast), eaten during the Passover festival.

MOSHAV (plural MOSHAVIM)
A farming community which is similar to a kibbutz, except that its members lead independent lives.

ORTHODOX JEW
Someone who keeps strictly to Jewish religious laws.

OTTOMAN TURKS
A Moslem people from Asia who conquered parts of south-east Europe, North Africa and the Middle East around 1520. They later lost part of this territory, but remained in control of the Middle East till 1917.

SEPHARDI
A term used to describe Jewish people from North Africa, the Mediterranean area and Arabic-speaking countries.

SHARAV
A hot, dry desert wind which blows from the south-east from May to mid-June and from September to October, filling the air with particles of sand. The Arabic name is "Khamsin".

SHERUT TAXI
A shared taxi which holds seven passengers and operates between two fixed points.

TERRACING
Cutting strips of farmland into the side of a hill, forming a pattern of "steps" in the hillside.

TORAH
A scroll containing the first five books of the Hebrew Bible.

ULTRA-ORTHODOX JEW
Someone who keeps strictly to Jewish religious laws, and also dresses in distinctive clothes. Men often study full-time in a religious centre.

WADI
A dry river-bed in the desert that may suddenly fill with water after a rainstorm.

WEST BANK
The area west of the River Jordan and the Dead Sea controlled by Israel after the 1967 war. Control of much of the area passed to the Palestinian National Authority in 1995.

ZIONISM
The Zionist movement was formed in the late 19th century to campaign for a Jewish homeland in the Middle Eastern area where the Israelites originally lived. "Zion" is another name for Jerusalem.

INDEX

SYRIA

LEBANON

GOLAN HEIGHTS

Metullah

Kiryat Shemona

Lake
Kinneret

Tiberias

Nazareth

Nahariya

Akko

NATIONAL WATER CARRIER

Jenin

○ Nablus

Tulkarem ○

Kalkilya ○

W E S T

B A N K

Ramallah

35°

Haifa

M E D I T E R R A N E A N

S E A

I S R A E L

Netanya

Petah
Tikva

Ramat
Gan

Tel Aviv
-Yafo

Rishon Le Zion

32°

150° 135° 120° 105° 90° 75° 60° 45° 30° 15° 0° 15° 30° 45° 60° 75° 90° 105° 120° 135° 150° 165° 180° 150°

75°

60°

45°

30°

15°

0°

15°

30°

45°